I0191112

Lessons in Transition
Enduring in Peace and Strength to Breakthrough

Lessons in Transition

Copyright © 2014 by Shantelle Love

All rights reserved. No part of this book may be reproduced or transmitted in any form or by any means, electronic or mechanical, including photocopying, recording or by any information storage and retrieval system, without written permission from the author, except for the inclusion of brief quotations in a review.

Dedication

This book is dedicated to my babies; Sachet, Brittani, Jordan, Elias II and Joshua. Without you, my life is truly incomplete. I love you. Also to the wonderful women that have taken on the role of mentor at different stages in my life, and there are many, I thank God for you. To my hilarious family, I love you more than words can say! You have cheered me on from day one! I pray I continue to make you proud. To my various cheerleaders and my stumbling blocks, thank you. Larran and Christyl, the knitting that took place in 2006 was ridiculously fantastic! God did that and with your love and guidance, I am here! Yes, 2014, I am here and God is still working on, in and through me. Mia, Mia!! You already know. I love you more than words can say!

To the pastors whose ministries have truly blessed me, I thank you so much for the timely Word that went forth out of your belly to a sista whose hunger for knowledge, Wisdom and understanding, has been quenched at each level and I have grown because of your dedication. Thank you for your service and obedience.

To the one who entered my life and forced me before God like never before; I truly know what, 'It was meant for evil, but God worked it for my good,' means. I'm stronger, I'm wiser, better and I am able to share the encounter and principles and lessons thereof.

With each relationship; each entrance and exit, I have learned and I am thankful that truly, ALL things indeed have worked together for my good.

This book represents lessons that I have learned over the last few years. I embarked on a journey of obedience and along that journey I have fallen, but I have gotten back up, alas, the journey continues.

Shantelle

Reviews

"Lessons In Transition is an awesome book for anyone wanting to discontinue repetitive cycles of what bad decisions bring into lives. Shantelle's transparency in her personal stories of failure and success help others create a life of freedom. Acknowledging past mistakes moves you toward the abundance God has for every area of your life. If you are honest with yourself while reading this book, you will begin to see the manifestations of what Wisdom, God's word and accountability will do for you in a positive way." ~ Christyl Benford, Singer, Songwriter and Digital Design Artist

"I appreciate the honest and candid direction the author provides in this wonderful summary of how each of us have a part in our life transitions. This book gives you a clear picture of the shortfalls or "root" areas that often keep us from moving to that next level or greater purpose that God already has for us.

It provides practical steps to line us back with God's original plan (word, prayer and accountability) and purpose for each of our lives. If you are looking for a plan to get your life back on track this book will help you to do that." ~ Mia Spring

"Lessons in Transition, is a positive, uplifting and inspirational tool for success. This is more than a book, but an interactive road map for anyone that wants to take back control of their life and inject positive change that will produce healthy and whole individuals through intentional accountability and progressive growth. I am confident that Lessons in Transition will do just that, help transition and forcefully motivate you to break the mold of repetitive habits that keep you from achieving your highest potential while thrusting you to reach and complete your divine destiny." ~ Larran Benford

Credits

Book Cover Design by Crystal Benford

Railroad picture credit to Leeroy of Lifepix

Bible References are New Living Translation (NLT) and Amplified Bible (AMP), *Biblegateway 2014*, unless otherwise noted.

Content of Jewels

Lessons in Transition
Enduring in Peace and Strength to Breakthrough

FORWARD

This book was born out of my foolishness and nonsense. You know - the stuff that makes mess messy. Thank God for his correction, no matter how painful. To be on Purpose's Path© is crucial…now I get it. Transition, is that place unknown, that place that is unfamiliar. To move in a manner where you can feel uneasy about the steps (you), but clear about the cause (purpose) There is a timing, a cadence and eloquence about the walk of transition; where your past doesn't even begin to define your ability.

It is my prayer that this little book will help you in your journey as you walk out the purpose *God* has for your life. Purpose is essential to our functioning and operating in our lives. How we behave, what we choose to do *does* matter. We are connected, we have influence and our actions are being judged by others. But, what really matters is, are we living the best life possible? Have we tapped into our purpose that has already been set forth before the foundations of this world were formed? Do you really know who you are?

The questions and an examination are extremely important as we make choices or are in circumstances not of our choosing, but with an understanding of purpose, we can not only see what is in front of us, but we can envision, at least in part, the outcome. This understanding can alleviate a lot of heartache and situations, where we made a choice. It can also alleviate stress, tension, doubt, fear and worry, even when we haven't made a particular choice - or at least a conscious choice.

Stay with me. I have learned some things in my life that I believe will help you as you navigate through the channels, tunnels, waters, valleys and over the mountains that show up as paths in your life. I believe that if we are taught a principle, and apply it practically, we will begin to understand its effectiveness. Even if it is a situation that we have not personally experienced, there are enough real-life tragedies to serve as great illustrations to keep our behavior modified to that which serves Christ, who in turn, serves us. "The Law was there to serve (protect) us, not for us to serve it." Bishop T.D. Jakes

I want to take you on my journey. I want to give you some tidbits of what I discovered on that journey. I will share some stories of my life, then, I will ask questions to find out if you have experienced a similar situation. In this process, I believe you will start to think critically about the choices you have made. You may have made choices based on fear, neglect, family values, etc.

It is **our choices** that end up defining our lives. Not our circumstances. If we are in Christ, He has promised to send us a guide, his Holy Spirit. But we must choose to listen to that still small voice, that unction or feeling that we get to do or ***not*** do something. *We must learn not to doubt, but to stay out of our own way.*

I hope this book challenges you in every area and on every level of your life. I pray that you will be blessed to gain insight that you didn't have. I pray that you have many, "Ah ha!" moments. I can honestly say that some things, opportunities and prayers were answered and looking right at me, but I couldn't "see" them. Having a correct perspective is a key component of understanding your purpose and ability to transition with Joy! Not always with ease, but with Joy!

Now let's walk this journey together.

Chapter 1

Perspective…
Do You See What I See?
Clearly Seeing Who God Created You to Be

Let's be honest, we have all had a skewed or incorrect perspective of something at some point. How many times were you absolutely certain that you saw or understood something, just to be wrong? What was the scenario? How did it make you feel? Go ahead, write it down below:

Perspective can be defined as: a way of regarding situations or topics etc., the **appearance** of things relative to one another as determined by their distance from the viewer. ~Visual Thesaurus, 2013

Well, I too, have had many times that I saw or judged a situation and was completely wrong. I am thinking about a situation when I was a thriving student in elementary school. I believe I was in 2nd or 3rd grade. I remember there was a teacher who was trying to pronounce my name. She bent over and asked, "Now say your name for me." I said, "Shaan-Telle." She said, "Ohhhh, Shant-Telle. Oh, you Shan't tell; ever. You won't say anything. I get it." Deer in headlights…**blink, blink, blink**. I didn't fully understand what she said or what she spoke into my fragile, very delicate spirit, but at that moment, I could *feel* something happen in my chest. I could feel, discouragement settling in, I could feel low self-esteem clothe itself around me. As she turned away from me and toward the other children, I remember going back to my desk, to observe the busy

1

classroom. I never said another word – until my mother surprised me and picked me up from school that day. I told her what the teacher said and I remember that was my last day at that school. I doubt that me telling her what the teacher told me, had any influence, but probably another life circumstance, she had to deal with, but I never saw that woman again; to my relief and for her betterment.

What I don't remember hearing is that "everything would be ok", and that my name actually means, *song*. What I didn't hear is that words *do* hurt; they matter, and to only believe that I will, shall and can speak with greatness and authority. Well, she was my mother and she would go to war for me and my brother, but because she was taught certain beliefs, she didn't counter it with encouraging words to *me*, but with a few *choice* words to that teacher. She handled that teacher, but missed an opportunity to dispel the spell.

This was the first act that I remember as being a defining moment in my life. It still stings, but only because I now realize the delay that belief and perspective has brought about in my life. Hmmm…I'm 43! I speak peace and release over that lady (she is probably long gone now as she was old as dust when I was that little girl) for speaking such vile hatred into the spirit of a little girl who would be influenced by her words. Released!

Here's the Lesson

Words *do* matter! Speak words of life to yourself *and* to others.

As I have gone through the years, I don't think about that moment, but it comes up in conversation and I believe that it is brought to my remembrance for two main reasons:

1. I never really thought to *deal* with it and

2. It will help someone else, hence the mention of it in this book.

Be careful of how you *choose* to view a particular situation. Now, in the scenario above, I was a little girl and I really didn't understand the importance of speaking positive affirmations. That is something that is taught, hence the many books filled with daily affirmations.

Hint; hint… your affirmation will be at the end of this chapter.

Be encouraged and use your voice! You are powerful! Your voice will open doors for not only you, but someone else, your voice will help **free** someone else. When you start having doubts about your ability, remember those thoughts do not come from our Heavenly Father, and they need to be cast down, set aside and dismissed!

Your perspective should provide clarity for your purpose. Even if you aren't sure of what your purpose is, stay tuned. We will go down that road as well.

Affirmation

I am clear that I was created to do, be and see great things! I am powerful and not pitiful! I am not hopeless! I see the world through bright eyes, through eyes that can see opportunity in any situation.

Scripture

For you created my innermost being, you knit me together in my mother's womb. I praise you because I am fearfully and wonderfully made; your works are wonderful, I know that full well. My frame was not hidden from you when I was made in the secret place. When I was woven together in the depths of the earth, your eyes saw my unformed body. All the days ordained for me were written in your book before one of them came to me. (NIV) Psalm 139.13-16

For Insight and Consideration

Pertaining to the situation that you wrote down, has your perspective changed? If so, how? If not, why?

What valuable lessons have you learned from your situation?

How can what you've learned help someone else?

How do you feel about sharing your story with others?

What would it mean to you if you let go of all your inhibitions, threw *caution* to the wind and just lived?

The Bible states to count the cost. What is it costing you to live a life that doesn't speak to what you have envisioned?

Chapter 2

Steal, Kill, and Destroy
What Does that Look Like?

So, I've heard this, but whaaat does this mean? I mean, how can I really understand what is killing me (except that maybe it's literal), steal – oh I have that one, I think. Destroy…hmmm.

Have you ever just had a conversation with yourself about something that totally perplexed you? Have you ever just sat back and listened to a conversation, even nodded, but had no clue as to what was being discussed? Well, I think that happens quite a bit with scripture references. Sometimes, we have just heard it so much, that we *think* we know. But we actually have no clue.

We often repeat things that we hear because it sounds good. It never really has to offer any substance and we don't have to understand it, but if we *feel* good after hearing it, then we just run with it. We respond to emotionalism – and that's dangerous. The Bible speaks of this in 2 Timothy 4:3:

> For the time will come when they will not endure sound doctrine; but after their own lusts shall they heap to themselves teachers, having itching ears; And they shall turn away their ears from the truth, and shall be turned unto fables.

This scripture speaks to us seeking to fulfill our desires, instead of coming into alignment with what the Word of God says and denying our flesh (what we want), reading and understanding what God has to say about a matter and lining up with that. We want to hear and succumb to what feels good. And we know that what always *feels* good is not necessarily *good for us*. There are times that we need to adhere to the principles and admonition of the Lord.

I don't know about you, but there are many times that I could have avoided a lot of foolishness and nonsense, had I not decided to go with my own program; you know…Chet Shantelle, written, directed and produced by…SELF! This is the worst program to be on since we can be unreasonable and unreliable in how we feel. We must depend on our faith to see us through and to give us strength to press through when we feel dismayed, depressed or deprived. Our faith keeps us focused on the vision or the end result and our feelings keep us focused on the current circumstances, which can change in an instant. Remain steady; do not look to the right or the left.

The goal of the enemy of your soul is to keep you focused on circumstances, disappointments, difficulties and other life challenges. That is what he will do to steal first, your joy. Then once your joy is gone he will attempt to kill your identity, by convincing you that you are nothing, but your identity is in Christ. Then ultimately keep you so distraught, he will distract you to the point of giving up and just sitting on the sidelines of *your* life, or whispering a lie to get you to walk an entirely different path other than what God intended.

Proverbs 4:20-27

My son, give attention to my words;
Incline your ear to my sayings.
^{21} Do not let them depart from your eyes;
Keep them in the midst of your heart;
^{22} For they *are* life to those who find them,
And health to all their flesh.
^{23} Keep your heart with all diligence,
For out of it *spring* the issues of life.
^{24} Put away from you a deceitful mouth,
And put perverse lips far from you.
^{25} Let your eyes look straight ahead,
And your eyelids look right before you.
^{26} Ponder the path of your feet,
And let all your ways be established.
^{27} Do not turn to the right or the left;
Remove your foot from evil.

Here's the Lesson

Stay focused on your goals, dreams, and visions. Get excited about the results you will produce and not the disappointments that will come because they will come. Learn from them and move on.

Just know that we all come from different backgrounds. Most of us never start from the same place. Know this truth: we all have the same grace. We have different vision, but the same love that flows from God to me, flows to you and vice versa. God desires our heart and when we draw nigh to Him, he allows us a closer, more intimate relationship with

Him. We grow in love, peace, patience, kindness, self-control, joy and faithfulness.

Affirmation

My eyes are opened to see all that God has for me. My discernment is keen and I have the ability to view things from a God perspective. I shall put on the full armor of God so that I will not be snared by the enemy.

Scripture

Finally, my brethren, be strong in the Lord and in the power of His might. [11] Put on the whole armor of God, that you may be able to stand against the wiles of the devil. [12] For we do not wrestle against flesh and blood, but against principalities, against powers, against the rulers of the darkness of this age,[a] against spiritual hosts of wickedness in the heavenly places. [13] Therefore take up the whole armor of God, that you may be able to withstand in the evil day, and having done all, to stand.

[14] Stand therefore, having girded your waist with truth, having put on the breastplate of righteousness, [15] and having shod your feet with the preparation of the gospel of peace; [16] above all, taking the shield of faith with which you will be able to quench all the fiery darts of the wicked one. [17] And take the helmet of salvation, and the sword of the Spirit, which is the word of God; [18] praying always with all prayer and supplication in the Spirit, being watchful to this end with all perseverance and supplication for all the saints— [19] and for me, that utterance may be given to me, that I may open my mouth boldly to make known

the mystery of the gospel, for which I am an ambassador in chains; that in it I may speak boldly, as I ought to speak. Ephesians 6:10-20

For Insight and Consideration

There are times when we all have had a *gut* feeling. When have you gone against that feeling?

Did you regret it? How So?

How has going against that feeling impacted the decision you were facing?

When have you gone with that *gut* feeling and knew that it was a great decision?

If you have made a decision that favored you, in discernment, have you ever gone against it again? If so, what has that taught you?

What do you take away from that experience?

Have you ever addressed your fears?

Chapter 3

The Pain Factor
The Pain of Remaining the Same

It all started when I wouldn't lower my expectations;
when I placed a demand on the integrity that he said
he upheld. When I said, "We agreed to…" or when I
called him on the carpet for behavior that was not
becoming of a Godly man or simply, a reasonable
man. It started when I made that request that the gifts
stop and the integrity of the man needed to shine; that
lying was unacceptable and how could you really say
that you love me and avoid the part where love
actually shows up? Well, in short, I met and married
more than just a hurting person, I married a person so
broken that he lived surrounding himself with other
people that would not only condone his behavior, but
assisted him in his behavior- his dysfunction. That's a
lot of blinded and broken people, but I *learned* that
there are more, many more that would hide in the
fabric of our families, churches, and communities –
and I met, dined, slept with, and did business with
many of them. So, what does that say about me?

Well, let's see…

The chosen dysfunctions, yes, the *chosen* ones are
keeping folks on lock with not only avoiding their
basic responsibilities to respect others, but to take a
keen look in the mirror at what stares back at them/us.
The fear of changing keeps people locked into an
unknown abyss for years! It's dealing with the same
issues over and over and over again. We can't resolve
anything we won't acknowledge. If we aren't

acknowledging our woes, ills, disappointments, etc., then we continue to live beneath our value. We deny that we even need help. We begin to mask the fact that under our everyday face; you know the one where we smile and say, "all is well", there are hidden wounds that need healing, *but, so many even deny the help to heal.*

If we would understand that help comes with accountability, then we would be able to recognize it when it's sent. We would be able to recognize the many people and opportunities that come our way, to give us a way out. We would recognize that beyond our pain there is hope. What we must understand is that no person comes to us without expecting us to change in some manner – even in our hearing or understanding. Yes, that is the accountability piece…we must be held accountable for saying we want something and our life speaks of something completely different. Here is where we get into trouble:

We begin to substitute healing with people, food, drugs, sex, anger, resentment, and other irrational attitudes and behaviors that not only deepen our wounds, but we end up inflicting that hurt onto others in our quest to avoid the responsibility to seek help, to heal. We end up with what I call, *healing deferred.* We delay our healing because it's too painful to acknowledge that we, yes, you and I are the problem and not everyone else. We deny that although there may have been less than ideal circumstances in our lives, that the responsibility to change lies solely with us. There *are* circumstances that happen to us, but it's the choices we make with what happened to us that will determine our outcome. I am not saying that there have not been some things that have happened in our youth or even in our adulthood that have not knocked the breath out of us, taken us by surprise, left us scarred, angry or even fearful, leery and deeply hurting. Those are all very real emotions that most of us have probably felt at one time or another. But if we are new creatures in Christ, then we should learn to live above our feelings by staying connected to the True Vine. Our feelings can get us into a lot of trouble. Our emotions, when not in context, can destroy us and override our ability to be effective in our lives, especially as it concerns Kingdom matters. There are times when we look around and all we see and experience is fear, doubt, despair, death, hopelessness, sarcasm, anger and resentment, to name a few. These are very real as well. That is why understanding your identity and having hope for a future because you understand that you were created with a purpose is essential. When we have a greater purpose, and we access that by envisioning our end, we can then place a demand on God, through prayer, to show us the path and provide the strategy and provision for accomplishing all that he set before us. We have rights as children of God and understanding who we are will give us a renewed energy.

Here's the lesson

Do not ignore the signs. Do not ignore the warnings. Stop seeing people that you are assigned to for a season in *their potential* and aligning with them in your future. You are assigned to their **NOW**. Congratulate them when they make progress and certainly when they arrive at destiny's door, but don't you dare marry the ministry! Stay focused on your assignment. We don't have time to be thwarted or enticed by satan's devices. We must grow in wisdom and discernment to stay the course and accomplish all that God would have us to in any particular season. We are on assignment, at all times, in every arena.

Affirmation

I am a child of God. I have purpose, I have something to say and do. I will accomplish all that God has set before me and not be distracted by the circumstances that surround me.

Scripture

"Before I formed you in the womb I knew you; before you were born I sanctified you; I ordained you a prophet to the nations."

~Jeremiah 1:5

For Insight and Consideration

How have you been resistant to change?

What fears do you have that you need to confront?

Identify the areas of dysfunction in your life. What are those areas and how can you begin to deal with them?

What does it cost you to remain the same?

What could you actually accomplish if fear wasn't a factor?

Have you identified the opportunities and people that are around you to hold you accountable? If so, how has that helped you? If not, are you willing to change your perspective so that you can see those that may benefit you?

Chapter 4

Bamboozled
I am Smarter than that!
Common Sense Does Not Equal Spiritual
Discernment

So I *thought* I was smarter than ***that***.

Well, we will see that head knowledge is no good in Kingdom matters. Wisdom, peace and discernment are key factors in decision making and avoiding the dangers, unseen. ~

2 Corinthians 10:4-6 - For the weapons of our warfare *are* not carnal but mighty in God for pulling down strongholds, [5] casting down arguments and every high thing that exalts itself against the knowledge of God, bringing every thought into captivity to the obedience of Christ, [6] and being ready to punish all disobedience when your obedience is fulfilled.

With that being said, there are times when we need to make quick decisions and we sometimes believe that making those sudden decisions are cause for concern. I have found that when my spirit is centered, saturated with the Word of God and I have been studying and reading, then I am prone to make sound judgments and decisions; even if they are sudden. We should seek wisdom daily from God and be ready when we need to think and act, quickly. In shifting our direction to match his, we align with his will and walk in purpose – on purpose!

I went out on *my own* so many times that I have lost count. I have entered into covenants and relationships that had nothing to do with God. They were my choosing; my doing. It's funny how we always want to get into something then cry for God to come and save us. "Get me outta this God and I won't do it again. Awww Lord, help me through this and I will never look back."

Yes, I have tried to make pacts with God, in my foolishness. We cannot bargain with God or with our purpose. Either we will get a clue about why we are on this earth to begin with and decide to align our thoughts and actions with that accordingly (allow God to drive) , or we will continue to live a deficient lifestyle, trying to figure it out; only to be left disappointed in the end. Oh sure, there were some days where I was all up in my flesh, living in sin and doing what would only momentarily or seasonally be satisfactory to me. I had to come to realize that if I wanted to truly be satisfied that I first had to simply be obedient. I *had* to listen to the Holy Spirit that was constantly calling to me. I had to surrender. I had to remove what I would understand to be stumbling blocks or distractions and they came in many, many forms. My own thoughts would attack me then doubt would come from others because after all, they *knew* me. Scenarios would be presented and I would be tempted to go along with them because I still had desires to do my own thing. My flesh was not dying because I was still lukewarm and although my faith was growing, I still trusted me and what I saw, rather than give it all to God for *my* good.

See, faith without works is truly dead. There is no faith if we don't leave our thinking (skewed and selfish) behind. If we are constantly battling with ourselves and always in a situation, we need to first address whether or not we are following Christ or following our minds apart from Christ. Yes, we are thinking creatures, we are supposed to be critical thinkers, but we are also, as followers of Jesus; supposed to have the mind of Christ (1 Corinthians 2:16). We should shed our "stinkin thinkin". You know; those thoughts that do you absolutely no good. Those thoughts that if left to marinade in the facets of your mind, will ultimately lead you to an action and eventually, regret. We will never, in our own ability, be able to navigate through this life and glean all of the Kingdom benefits that we are entitled to on this earth as joint heirs with Christ. We must challenge our thoughts and cast them aside as scripture reminds us in 2 Corinthians 10:5-7 and in Philippians 4:8. Replace thoughts that do not line up with God's word with those that do. It's that simple.

It has been my experience that distractions become deterrents when we don't fully understand our purpose. It's not the walk oftentimes that is daunting, we deal with trials every day and in many areas of our lives, it's the lack of clarity we have concerning our actual purpose we and the *why* that is attached to the walk that gives us pause. We often wonder whyyyy this, or whyyyy that? Why am I doing this when it gets hard or why should I continue if no one is here to support me? Why do this when I don't know what is at the end of the tunnel, the rainbow, the end? Why? What's the use?

Let's get clear. Oftentimes, we will not understand the full impact our purpose has on the people around us, much less how it affects us. That is when our focus needs to change. We need to redirect our energy toward the One who called us to the purpose and make a decision that we will be obedient, no matter what! We will die doing what we know we are supposed to do even if the answers never come, even if we don't feel appreciated or worthy or 'up to it'. We must decide that the *obedience* attached to our call is far more important that our understanding of it is. This is where we press! This is where we fight our flesh and our emotions, our family and friends perceptions of us and even our perceptions of ourselves, to march on! Keep going. This is what I call having a *laser focus*. This is where we challenge our soul to line up with the spirit realm and really be overcomers.

Here's the Lesson

Our thinking must line up with the Word of God if we are going to walk in our purpose and reap all of the benefits. Our purpose will not only bless us, but so many others; even in our process of falling down and getting back up. The battlefield is in the mind. Get the mind renewed and the process of walking out your purpose becomes clear. As you see purpose, each step is a reminder of your *why* and enables you to continue no matter the stumbling blocks that come your way.

Affirmation

I will not be delayed by being in denial. I will seek my purpose and walk in that purpose; determined not to be distracted and disobedient. My focus is clear and I will not be denied.

Scripture

For we are God's workmanship, created in Christ Jesus to do good works, which God prepared in advance for us to do. Ephesians 2:10

For Insight and Consideration

Think back to a time you have ignored your intuition. When did you recognize that you should have gone with your "first mind"?

How did ignoring that impact that particular situation?

Why have you not trusted that voice that was telling you to *do* or *not* do something?

How would you describe your choices regarding your major life circumstances thus far?

What did/would it take for you to start to trust you?

Why do you think you doubt your spiritual discernment?

Chapter 5

The Other Side of 'Why'
The Error and Ignorance of Knowing

I knew not to walk down that road. I *knew* when I said 'yes' and *not* 'no' that I would be disappointed. I prayed and asked God for direction and when I "knew" my answer showed up - well, actually I *knew* that what was sent was not my answer, but I needed to know *whyyyyy wasn't* he it, why wasn't that thing or whatever the object of my prayed for desire; my answer? Why couldn't I have what I wanted and what was obviously sent? Why when I ask *why* does it take so long to get an answer? Why would this choice be so bad? Why should I ignore *this* and move on to *that*?

There would be many times that I knew not to ask, *why* or *why not*? But, I insisted on an answer and my flesh had to be satisfied in *its* knowing. My spirit was crying aloud as I ignored the most dependable part of me to simply... Leave. It. Alone. And trust God.

When a door closes, that is an opportunity to assess where you are *at **that** moment*. Become conscious of the distractions in your environment and be determined to stay focused, no matter the cost. When we get clear about our purpose and begin to see the *impact* of our purpose, we will not stop at anything to ensure that it is accomplished. When we stop to give anything that is not designed to push us forward, we believe we must know why that person, situation, job, tool, business, etc., is not for us.

Do you ever remember asking your parents if you could go stay overnight at a friend's or relative's house and your answer was a resounding, "NO"? I remember thinking that my mother was just mean and wanted us to be miserable staying in the house, watching our little black and white TV, reading the same old books, or playing with the same old stuff! Ugh!!! We were SO deprived, or so I thought. While everyone else was going to the sleepover, we were made to stay home. We couldn't indulge and do what other children were doing. Geesh, they were having fun and their parents didn't seem to care what they did. They were the group to follow.

Yeah right.

Well, I was one to always want an explanation as to why this and why that? If I couldn't do something, I wanted to know, why? It never settled with me to know that my feelings of deprivation would go unanswered when there stood an answer. A group of my peers hanging out and I could be a part, if only my mother would listen to my reasonably intelligent 10-year old mind. But she wasn't reasoning with a 10-year old. Hmmm…the answer was usually, "because I said so." Awww, that would make my skin crawl and I would be more determined to argue my point.

Until.

Until, I was threatened with a spanking or being sent to my room and being deprived of the things I had access to even there. So, I shut up, but with no understanding.

But oh my mother caved one day when I pleaded with her to let me go to a friend's house, with promises that the parents would be home, they had an actual house, they were responsible and hey, Michelle was the prettiest and second smartest girl in class (I was the head class act…wink), and hey, she had two parents, we were going to be fed, and she could get rid of me overnight. Well, she gave in.

I remember that I called her in the middle of the night to come and get me. I remember that there was a cousin, who I view in retrospect, had some issues and was molesting the group of girls at my friend's house. She was a teenage girl, obviously with issues that either her family denied or didn't know were there. When I called my mother, she simply stated, "I'm on my way and I knew you would call." I told her what happened and declared that I would *never* ask why I couldn't do something again. I was safe and unharmed.

When my mother picked me up, she notified the parents and let's just say, my friend wasn't allowed to speak to me anymore and even she didn't understand why.

While my mother was angry at the situation, and possibly for even giving in to my rants about wanting to go to a house she knew nothing about, she was also relieved that I was safe. I believe that if I would have even thought to ask about another sleepover, I wouldn't be writing this today (smile). Momma would have taken me out!

Her responsibility was to protect and to provide for me. She never owed me an explanation of *why*? Any explanation that she gave my little mind could not have comprehended in that season of my life. I couldn't prioritize bills and other necessities, when choices had to be made regarding our safety and welfare, so when the choices had to be made, she didn't offer sympathies or explanations, she did what she *had* to do and was *supposed* to do. It was love and mostly fun growing up with her and the times when I was obedient, without taking her through changes, the rewards were sweet. Peace and no chastisement, no correction. It was for the benefit of not only me, but our family and our community.

Oftentimes, God will protect us much in the same manner. Only He can see the end from the beginning, he created us in his image for a set time and purpose on this earth. Who better to know what we need and how to get it to us? Even when we go our own way, grace covers us and is sufficient. What a wonderful, powerful protective God we serve! If we would only align our thoughts with his and know that in ordering our steps, uh hello, he *must* be the leader! When we are determined to do things our way, on our own, then He will say, "Ok". We get free will. We get to choose. When we are ready to listen, he is always ready to receive us. But at what cost do we walk in our own limited senses and understanding? What time has it cost us? How have we been unnecessarily wounded?

God provides protection and provision for us *when we receive it*. It's that simple. When we are always seeking *why* and *how come*... and God continues to allow a situation to evade our understanding; that is a clue to keep moving. Stop trying to open closed doors, making a square peg fit into a round hole, justify gross stupidity and sin and attempting to comprehend that which is simply not for you. Stop it! It's like eating of the tree of good and evil in The Garden of Eden! By the time you realize what you have done, you have set yourself, your family, friends and others who have been waiting on your contribution to them all the way back. You have destroyed the word of your testimony and cast a shadow on the Word of God! There are certain things we don't need to know. There are certain situations we absolutely cannot handle and there are times when we just need to avoid our own senses and just go with the Leading of the Holy Spirit. Let God rule in our hearts, walk in obedience and appreciate the Holy Spirit and our angels for their protection and direction.

Here's the Lesson

Sometimes, our protection comes as we sleep, as we are unaware. That is the best protection – when we are unaware of its process, but aware of the benefits, regardless of how we *feel*.

Affirmation

God has placed the spirit of discernment in me. I do not need any person's approval. I will not continue to self-sabotage myself and delay my future by being in denial of this truth and power. The God in me is enough!

Scripture

Behold, I stand at the door and knock; if anyone hears and listens to and heeds My voice and opens the door, I will come in to him and will eat with him, and he [will eat] with Me. Revelation 3:20

Now the serpent was more subtle and crafty than any living creature of the field which the Lord God had made. And he [Satan] said to the woman, Can it really be that God has said you shall not eat from every tree of the garden?

² And the woman said to the serpent, We may eat the fruit from the trees of the garden,

³ Except the fruit from the tree which is in the middle of the garden. God has said, You shall not eat of it, neither shall you touch it, lest you die.

⁴ But the serpent said to the woman, You shall not surely die,

⁵ For God knows that in the day you eat of it your eyes will be opened, and you will be like God, knowing the difference between good and evil and blessing and calamity.

⁶ And when the woman saw that the tree was good (suitable, pleasant) for food and that it was delightful to look at, and a tree to be desired in order to make one wise, she took of its fruit and ate; and she gave some also to her husband, and he ate.

[7] Then the eyes of them both were opened, and they knew that they were naked; and they sewed fig leaves together and made themselves apronlike girdles.

[8] And they heard the sound of the Lord God walking in the garden in the cool of the day, and Adam and his wife hid themselves from the presence of the Lord God among the trees of the garden.

[9] But the Lord God called to Adam and said to him, Where are you?

[10] He said, I heard the sound of You [walking] in the garden, and I was afraid because I was naked; and I hid myself.

[11] And He said, Who told you that you were naked? Have you eaten of the tree of which I commanded you that you should not eat?

[12] And the man said, The woman whom You gave to be with me—she gave me [fruit] from the tree, and I ate.

[13] And the Lord God said to the woman, What is this you have done? And the woman said, The serpent beguiled (cheated, outwitted, and deceived) me, and I ate.

[14] And the Lord God said to the serpent, Because you have done this, you are cursed above all [domestic] animals and above every [wild] living thing of the field; upon your belly you shall go, and you shall eat dust [and what it contains] all the days of your life.

[15] And I will put enmity between you and the woman, and between your offspring and her [a]Offspring; He

will bruise and tread your head underfoot, and you will lie in wait and bruise His heel.

¹⁶ To the woman He said, I will greatly multiply your grief and your suffering in pregnancy and the pangs of childbearing; with spasms of distress you will bring forth children. Yet your desire and craving will be for your husband, and he will rule over you.

¹⁷ And to Adam He said, Because you have listened and given heed to the voice of your wife and have eaten of the tree of which I commanded you, saying, You shall not eat of it, the ground is under a curse because of you; in sorrow and toil shall you eat [of the fruits] of it all the days of your life.

¹⁸ Thorns also and thistles shall it bring forth for you, and you shall eat the plants of the field.

¹⁹ In the sweat of your face shall you eat bread until you return to the ground, for out of it you were taken; for dust you are and to dust you shall return.

²⁰ The man called his wife's name Eve [life spring], because she was the mother of all the living.

²¹ For Adam also and for his wife the Lord God made long coats (tunics) of skins and clothed them.

²² And the Lord God said, Behold, the man has become like one of Us [the Father, Son, and Holy Spirit], to know [how to distinguish between] good and evil and blessing and calamity; and now, lest he put forth his hand and take also from the tree of life and eat, and live [b] forever—

²³ Therefore the Lord God sent him forth from the Garden of Eden to till the ground from which he was taken.

²⁴ So [God] drove out the man; and He placed at the east of the Garden of Eden the ^[c]cherubim and a flaming sword which turned every way, to keep and guard the way to the tree of life.

For Insight and Consideration

When Wisdom shows up, do you listen or do your choose to go your own way? How do you recognize Wisdom?

How do you challenge yourself to renew your mind?

When do you consciously tell yourself to stop, drop and move in a different direction?

Who is your accountability partner? Do you have different partners for different instances in your life? Can you recognize what is has cost you as you've asked, why?

How has this impacted others in your life?

How have you been wounded as you asked, why?

Have you healed? How? Write the steps you have taken.

Chapter 6

Forgiveness
There is No Justice in Revenge

When you hold unforgiveness in your heart, it becomes breeding ground for bitterness.

We have an awesome opportunity to empty our hearts of past hurts and walking into new relationships with the warmth, love and enthusiasm that we did when we "fell" the first time, if we would admit the pain. Own our part or what I call owning your stuff, accepting the resolve that was offered and moving on. That resolve may not be what we expected. The person may have walked out, unapologetically, lied, berated us or left us for dead; forgive them!
Any unanswered questions? Leave them. The resolve is that what happened should be a lesson and an opportunity to learn, grow and pass on information out of the love of your heart, not the bitterness that manifests.

Oftentimes, we are ruled by our emotions and soul components, instead of being led by our spirit that should line up with what and who God says we are. When we can assess a situation from the viewpoint of healing, rather than hurting, our perspective becomes clear and we don't seek to offend another, but can love them even when we have been wronged.
There *are* times where we will want to demand an explanation from the one who offended, but when someone offends, is "I'm sorry" or "I apologize" enough, especially; if it's bordered by the fact that the relationship is over? There are some things we must

resolve to simply, let go. First, we let go of negative emotions. We should not let anyone or any situation take us out of our God nature. The Bible speaks about keeping our emotions under our feet. We should be led by truth no matter the situation. Our emotions have a place and that is why we were given them. We use them to be empathetic, sympathetic, loving, to admire and even to be angry.

Forgiveness is not optional. It provides us the freedom we need to approach God in our fallen state, when we need intercession. We must allow God to provide justice on our behalf. He will pay recompense.

More than waiting and holding our breath for someone to come back and apologize for something they cannot understand or see is wrong, we must begin to make better choices and decisions. When we lower our expectations and align with those who are not a part of our destiny, we discount our own value. Remember, we are created in the image of God. Set standards and then we aren't so quick to be wounded. When people hurt you, let them know and if need be, let them go.

Affirmation

I will forgive those who have hurt me and pray for those who have used me. This is to my benefit and my freedom lies in my ability to truly forgive. I hold no hostages.

Here's the Lesson

We have a responsibility to heal. Period. Wounded Warriors refers to those who have been wounded, but have rested, reflected and healed. They don't go on contaminating others and activate through hurt and hate. Those are people full of pride. If we are filled with trash from previous relationships we become drugged with woes and transfer that energy and false "truths" from a skewed perspective, instead of one filled with hope.

Scripture

For if you forgive men when they sin against you, your heavenly Father will also forgive you. But if you do not forgive men their sins, your Father will not forgive your sins.~ Matthew 6:14-15

Repent, then, and turn to God, so that your sins may be wiped out, that times of refreshing may come from the Lord, ~Acts 3:19

And when you stand praying, if you hold anything against anyone, forgive him, so that your Father in heaven may forgive you your sins. ~Mark 11:25

For Insight and Consideration

What issues of bitterness do you need to examine in your life?

Who do you need to forgive? Why?

At the times you find yourself wanting to "get back" at someone, how do you diffuse your thoughts? Have you identified your triggers with regards to holding onto forgiveness?

How has holding onto forgiveness impeded your progress toward healing?

If you have identified areas in your life that need to be healed, can you state the steps that were taken to get you to your place of freedom? If so, state those below:

If not, then I challenge you to start writing down the steps that you have taken to heal.

Chapter 7

You're "Ah-ha" Moment
When the Light Comes On, Pay Attention!

Whew! Have you ever had a moment where you nearly fell over because a thought or a remembrance of something *clicked*? No really, you nearly caused a pile up in as you would suddenly halt in a hallway at work, sighed deeply or screamed out of nowhere because something *finally* made sense? Of course you have! We all have.

Well, I've had those moments and I find that it is my mind being renewed. Those are the times that I feel God has added a puzzle piece he knows I can handle, and it gives me added direction for my walk.

Clarity. There is nothing like it. Retrospect and hindsight are key elements and clues to help you along the way.

For me, writing in a journal is necessary. It's not optional. When I don't have my journal with me, then I use a recording device. It's important that we keep record of our steps. Keeping records will remind us of our goal, our purpose, our reason for doing, the mistakes that we have made, the falling down and getting up and we are able to see our "snapshots" as a whole picture. We can course correct, if you will, and make better decisions. We aren't so quick to forget, and our story is transparent, as it is on paper. We can also share with others our *who, what, when, where, how* and yes, *why*.

At times, we can look at what we have written and begin to see patterns that we need to break or habits that we need to continue. We can see areas that we need to develop and be open to understanding that if we stay the course, progress will come.

I've had more than one "aha" moment, too many to count. One moment came when I decided to move from Austin back to Colorado. I was moving because I thought I was going to go back, marry the love of my life, open a spa and show off my immaculate massage skills, write poetry and continue to raise my kids and take on the role of step- mommy.

Oh how wrong I would be. I moved back and if I could tell you how quickly my plans changed and how what I identified as my best, could have been the worst mistake of my life…. I was truly saved by the bell, saved by grace and not because of wisdom, but rejection. It was subtle, but so profound and necessary. I didn't know that I was being *called* back. I had to go back and be introduced to my life as God saw it. I also had to receive what was being handed to me. I was sent back to start over, to start fresh and to start new.

I stepped into a position at a company, was introduced to people, I would not otherwise meet. I was invited by my now, sister (not natural, but better), to meet her husband and attend a local church. It was under the tutelage of that pastor, and support of all of the members, that I would start to get a glimpse of my identity in Christ. I would begin to understand that what I could see spiritually was not unusual or "abnormal".

Scream!!!

I wasn't alone and I started to develop by surrounding myself with those who had similar experiences and callings. I would also begin to separate from those that were there as stones to help catapult me into purpose. These weren't necessarily easy times, but the *process,* the feeding and growth caused me to smile and as I nodded my head and the light came on, I smiled and, "aha" was exactly what I said. It was clear that every step, every action, every person was sent by God to help me go back to move forward. Ha!

I don't know about you, but when I begin to understand something, without asking, *why*, when God just reveals, by his spirit (1 Corinthians 2:7) I am so fulfilled. It's the unexpected blessing in revelation. The Word illuminates and provides a lamp unto our feet and light unto our path (Psalm 119:105). We can continue as our why (purpose) continues to be revealed.

During these times, we need to stay focused, humble so that we can be corrected when necessary and quickly complete each task set before us, so that our faith can grow and doubt can be laid aside.

I was called, accepted the call, filled, trained, supported, ordained and sent back into the field to continue as God would provide the provision, protection and guidance as I continued to allow him and not get in my own way. I would truly start to understand my purpose in the field, in the wilderness, in the unknown. I would begin to understand how unique this walk is and how important the journey is. I would begin to see the significance of obedience, the courage and power of a "yes" and how being set apart, inclines my ear to sharpen and my words to shape what is in the spirit but must manifest in the natural. I started to "get it". The delays, the detours, the relationships, the tears, the joy and the exchange of what my soul longed for versus what my spirit required.

Aha! Now I get it!

I would recover from my mistakes quicker and I would take greater risks and harder falls. I just wouldn't stay out of place long. I am now desperate to reach my goals and be a purpose filled, on fire, set-apart sista! My spirit grieves when I'm out of alignment. My aha's are beneficial as I can stay the course and have validation for the progress. They are seeds planted for a greater harvest.

I suspect many of you have had similar experiences. My prayer is that you will grow and mature during these times. Look for those moments and celebrate by doing whatever is being dictated, in that moment, in that season.

Affirmation

Even when I don't see the desired results, I refuse to quit. I will take all of my "aha" moments and choose to use them as seeds and I will eventually see my harvest.

Here's the Lesson

Use those "Ah-ha" moments as stepping stones. You will be able to build a wealth of knowledge and understanding, while minimizing making the same and similar mistakes.

Scripture

For I know the thoughts and plans that I have for you, says the Lord, thoughts and plans for welfare and peace and not for evil, to give you hope in your final outcome. Jeremiah 29:11

For Insight and Consideration

Write down your "aha" moment.

What did you do when you had the revelation?

How would you say that moment helped to define where you are now?

Did you share this with anyone else?

Chapter 8

My Purpose
Who Am I?

I wished I knew then what I know now. How many times have you made *that* statement? I've thought about that more times than I care to mention.

As I stated in the previous chapter, I had so much revelation at one point that I have wondered, *what if?* You know how we wonder how far along we could have been had we understood more, had we done things differently?

Well, my purpose unfolded after I got into position. I was already operating in my purpose, but the clarity of what I was to do and who I would encounter was only relevant after I got into position. What does that mean?
That meant that I had to be willing to leave behind what was once comfortable and familiar and delve off into what would be a wilderness experience. I left my job, friends, family and even my daughters (my sons came with me), to be obedient to what was already sown and revealed in my spirit. So much happened on that journey, that I can truly say that if my *faith* had not been intact, I would have turned around and gone home. I would have just given up, because what I saw *and* experienced would have been enough for anyone with two sets of eyes on her to turn around and just go back to what was familiar and comfortable; to both me and my sons!

But when you are operating in purpose, you choose to not only believe God, you go in the midst of all the chaos and hell that would come your way and try to discourage you from moving forward. There were people that I fully expected to support me, start speaking doubt and fear, because somehow, my (physical) absence would result in the disappointment of their distorted perspective of my capabilities. And while it's true that *I* am not that cool, what was missing is the fact, that holding onto God's everlasting arm, is what was carrying me. It was not my choosing on my own, but my desire to be where I was supposed to be and do what I was supposed to do. Thankfully, those desires lined up EXACTLY as God would have them to.

You see, as I was packing up to come, the enemy was doing his best to discourage me by the phone call that I wasn't going to be able to purchase a home because the mortgage company I was working with online, was small and the mortgage crises had just really started. Then, on the advice of my realtor at the time, I decide to rent an apartment until I could get approved through another company and look for a house. Well, that didn't work out because while we were driving a 20 ft. truck, on the road to Texas, I get a phone call from the complex telling me that they couldn't rent from me because there was something on my credit report from a previous complex. Hmmmm…really? I rented from three previous private owners and had no issues there.
Oh, then there was the fact that the truck broke down three times….lol! We got lost and a 15 hr. trip turned into 25 hrs.

Here is where things turned around.

After I got the call from the apartment complex that they would not rent to me, with callousness, I cannot begin to explain, annnd after receiving payment and paperwork two weeks prior, I get a call from a friend who simply asked, "Hey stranger, I thought you were moving to Texas?" I wanted to scream! But instead, I explained that I was actually on the highway, with the boys and had just gotten the phone call about the apartment. Isn't God awesome! He put me on someone's mind and I hadn't spoken to in over a year!

A very long story short: We made it safely (I had never driven anything that big with a car towed on the back – hot mess!) and about 40 days later… God not only blessed me with an agent who was a Believer, but who listened to what I said and what I didn't, I closed on a home that only God could have placed in my path! Yes, I found, or better stated, I was directed to a home, closed, got money back, for being diligent and obedient.

It was not me. I couldn't have been so wise and had all of the pieces come together like they did. That was God in his infinite wisdom.

My purpose journey continues and in this position, I have learned:

~You absolutely *cannot* go by what it looks like.

~Faith and obedience are the keys to unlocking revelation.

~Strategy in Kingdom matters is essential.

~Trust and Believe God only!

This walk is not over, this is truly the beginning. This happened in 2008, so take it for what you will. My new beginning and fresh revelation has been enlightening. Fresh wind was breathed into me and fresh oil was poured *on* me. Everything that I needed for this season of my journey was already provided. Right down to the house and community that I would be in.

Affirmation

I am the apple of God's eye. I have a responsibility to be a change agent here in the earth realm. I cannot understand my purpose, if I don't first understand who God is and why I was created. The God I serve is the author and finisher of my faith and if I stand with him, he will watch over me, even when I fall, to ensure that the plans for my life will come to fruition.

Here's the Lesson

Purpose is essential and it begins with identity. Period.

Scripture

Looking away [from all that will distract] to Jesus, Who is the Leader and the Source of our faith [giving the first incentive for our belief] and is also its Finisher [bringing it to maturity and perfection]. He, for the joy [of obtaining the prize] that was set before Him, endured the cross, despising and ignoring the

shame, and is now seated at the right hand of the
throne of God. ~Hebrews 12:2

For Insight and Consideration

Are you operating in the area of purpose? Why or
why not?

If you are, at what point was your purpose made clear
to you?

If you aren't, have you prayed and asked God to show
you?

How does your purpose help others?

Chapter 9

The Trauma of Transition
Wilderness Experience

Transition: n. an event that occurs when something passes from one state or phase to another
v. change the nature, purpose of function of something

You *must* move! There is a place, region, position, area that you are supposed to be in. Now get to that place – quickly!

Truly, there is, to some degree or another, anxiety as we move to a new place, enter a new workplace, meet in-laws or are introduced to any new situation in our lives. There is anticipation and thoughts of, "who, what where when and how?" Transition is difficult for some and seemingly easy for others. The idea of coming into something new for the first time can cause major anxiety and even depression for some people. On the other hand, the idea of transition is viewed as new opportunities for others. A chance to meet new people, using newly acquired skills or learning new skills.

Transition should be viewed as an open door, a pathway to the '*new*'.

Although we don't always know what lies (exactly) in the transition, we should have a clear perception of purpose and at the very least, know that whatever takes place in the transition, it's there to further develop us in our purpose and strengthen us in the process.

There have been many times that I have wanted to scream as I went through a door that I *knew* I was supposed to walk through, and screamed because *my* idea of what was to happen, was almost instantly ruined. I have always thought of myself as giving. You know, going in and just pouring out all of your love, knowledge, wisdom and intellect for others to digest. Yeah, that's me.

However, in transition, as indicated in the definition; there *should* be a change. And as in all changes, it should begin with you, the image that looks back at you in the mirror. Yes, Believers should enter an atmosphere and expect to convert the atmosphere by using our authority in Christ. However, before we can illicit change, we must first **be** the change.

As we think of transition, we can think of our thinking. The Bible speaks about a renewed mind (Romans 12:2) and aligning our will to our God, our source of transformation. Our thoughts control our actions. We must be very careful of the things we choose to process in our thoughts. Negative images will store in our heart and then we end up speaking our fears, if we are always focusing on lack, death, stress and everything contrary to the Word of God. We store images, whether we are conscious of it or not. That is why the Bible is clear on what things we should *think* about

For the rest, brethren, whatever is true, whatever is worthy of reverence and is honorable and seemly, whatever is just, whatever is pure, whatever is lovely and lovable, whatever is kind and winsome and

gracious, if there is any virtue and excellence, if there is anything worthy of praise, think on and weigh and take account of these things [fix your minds on them].
~ Philippians 4:8

We should always use scripture as our barometer, our source of reference. For the Word never changes as does the times, our emotions, environment, relationships and even our outlook. We grow and develop and (hopefully) mature as we get older. There is only one Solid Rock we can stand on as we transition and unfold our purpose and path.

It takes courage and a dependency on the Word of God to be established in our lives, so that when the winds and storms of life come, we are not knocked completely off course. When we get turned around, we always can course correct. If we are operating in purpose, we should always be transitioning and making sure that we are aligning with what the word of God says. Sure, we can get discouraged, but we don't stay in that place. We have too much to do, so we must move. People full of purpose, cannot, and will not sit still. Idle and busy work is *not* what we do.

Affirmation

I am responsible for doing and being all that God has called me to be. I will reposition myself by renewing my mind and moving into the area that God has destined for me. I will die empty of all of the gifts deposited within me.

Here's the Lesson

Water that sits ultimately starts to stink and mold. Movement of that water serves to soothe, support, nourish or cleanse. The same is true about us. If we sit still, we will ultimately die and lose sight of hope and vision. Our sight becomes blurry and oftentimes regret, despair and bitterness sets in. Do not allow fear and unbelief keep you from your destiny and promise. Live this life knowing that we only have God, not man, to please. Allow *purpose* to be your focus.

Scripture
For God did not give us a spirit of timidity (of cowardice, of craven and cringing and fawning fear), but [He has given us a spirit] of power and of love and of calm and well-balanced mind and discipline and self-control.~ 2 Timothy 1:7

For Insight and Consideration

Who does **God** say you are? (Read Jeremiah 29:11)

What fears do you have regarding obedience and the cause for Christ?

www.ingramcontent.com/pod-product-compliance
Lightning Source LLC
Chambersburg PA
CBHW071933020426
42331CB00010B/2853